DATE DUE			

GARETH STEVENS
VITAL SCIENCE
Earth Science

BIOMES AND ECOSYSTEMS

by Barbara J. Davis
Science curriculum consultant: Suzy Gazlay, M.A.,
science curriculum resource teacher

Gareth Stevens
Publishing

Please visit our Web site at: www.garethstevens.com
For a free color catalog describing Gareth Stevens Publishing's list of high-quality books,
1-800-542-2595 (USA) or 1-800-387-3178 (Canada).
Gareth Stevens Publishing's fax: (877) 542-2596

Library of Congress Cataloging-in-Publication Data

Davis, Barbara J.
   Biomes and ecosystems / Barbara J. Davis.
     p. cm. — (Gareth Stevens vital science - earth science)
   Includes bibliographical references and index.
   ISBN-10: 0-8368-7761-6   ISBN-13: 978-0-8368-7761-8 (lib. bdg.)
   ISBN-10: 0-8368-7872-8   ISBN-13: 978-0-8368-7872-1 (softcover)
   1. Biotic communities—Juvenile literature.   I. Title.
   QH541.14.D38   2007
   577—dc22   2006033114

This edition first published in 2007 by
Gareth Stevens Publishing
A Weekly Reader® Company
1 Reader's Digest Rd.
Pleasantville, NY 10570-7000 USA

This edition copyright © 2007 by Gareth Stevens, Inc.

Produced by White-Thomson Publishing Ltd.
Editor: Walter Kossmann
Designer: Melissa Valuch
Photo researcher/commissioning editor: Stephen White-Thomson
Gareth Stevens editorial direction: Mark Sachner
Gareth Stevens editor: Leifa Butrick
Gareth Stevens art direction: Tammy West
Gareth Stevens production: Jessica Yanke and Robert Kraus

Science curriculum consultant: Tom Lough, Ph.D., Associate Professor of Science Education,
Murray State University, Murray, Kentucky

Illustrations by Peter Bull Art Studio
Photo credits: CORBIS, p. 22 (© Martin Harvey/Gallo Images); I-Stock, pp. 4 (both),
5 (both) 7, 8 (both), 9, 15, 16, 20, 23, 24, 25, 27, 29, 32, 33, 36 (both), 37 (both), 38,
cover and 39, title page and 43, 44; NHPA, pp. 9 (Daniel Heuclin), 10 (Andy Rouse),
21 (Martin Wendler); OSF, pp. 31 (Phototake, Inc.), 41 (Stan Osolinski).

Cover: An elephant and calf in the Kenya savanna need an extensive area as an
ecosystem to find food and water.
Title page: A coral reef provides food and shelter for a large number of sea creatures.

Printed in the United States of America

1 2 3 4 5 6 7 8 9 10 10 09 08

TABLE OF CONTENTS

1 INTRODUCTION

The world is full of living and nonliving things. A concrete sidewalk and the soil beneath it are examples of nonliving parts of an environment. Plants, animals, and human beings are examples of living things. All day, every day, the living and nonliving parts of the world interact and affect each other. These continual interactions take place in Earth's ecosystems and biomes.

What Is an Ecosystem?

An ecosystem can be very small, like a puddle of pond water or a decaying log in a forest. It can also be large, like the Florida Everglades. Regardless of size, the living and nonliving parts of an ecosystem can be helpful, or sometimes harmful, to that ecosystem. For example, encouraging bats to live in an area might help control the disease-carrying mosquito population because bats eat mosquitoes. Burning vast areas of forest for farmland, however, can hurt the quality of air we breathe—even if the forest is half a world away.

What Is a Biome?

A biome is a group of ecosystems that share certain characteristics. The characteristics are usually defined in broad terms of climate and rainfall. Warm temperatures and very little rainfall describe a desert biome. Warm temperatures and a lot of rainfall describe a rain forest biome.

Ecosystems and biomes can be viewed as a series of connections. Plants, animals, rocks, and rain—everything in an ecosystem or a biome is connected in

▲ The beaver, water, trees, and all other things in this ecosystem are connected.

▲ The Everglades in Florida is a vast ecosystem that is home to hundreds of unusual plant and animal species. Human activity, such as farming or home building, has reduced the Everglades to about half its original size. Many people now realize the importance of the Everglades ecosystem, and steps are being taken to preserve this natural treasure.

▲ The Namibia Desert in southwestern Africa is a typical desert biome. Although it looks lifeless, a desert biome can support a variety of plant and animal life.

ome way. Changing how parts of an ecosystem or a biome connect may have long-range effects. A permanent change in the amount of rainfall in an area affects the amount of water available for plants and animals. Without enough water, the soil dries out, plants and animals die off, and the ecosystem changes.

This book is about ecosystems and biomes and the organisms that depend on them for survival. Human beings are an extremely important part of ecosystems and biomes, so the role of people in Earth's systems will be explored. The connections that exist between all things on Earth will also be explored. The saying "We're all in this together" might be considered the theme of this book, because we are!

2 ECOSYSTEMS

The *eco* in the word *ecosystem* comes from the Greek word *oikos*, which means "house." Ecosystems can be thought of as everything that makes up the house, as well as the organisms that live there. For the tiny, shrimplike krill and the whales that eat them, the house is made up of salt water and microscopic plankton. For a cactus wren or a scorpion, the house includes dry sand and thick-skinned desert plants. Whether it is a place that is frozen most of the year or one where rainfall is a daily occurrence, an ecosystem is a place where all the organisms within it live.

Ecosystems' Components

Ecosystems include both biotic (living) and abiotic (nonliving) components. (Components are smaller parts that combine to make up something larger. In this case, the parts come together to make up an ecosystem.) All of the ecosystem's components are connected in some way. In a forest ecosystem, biotic components include everything from microscopic bacteria to delicate mosses to trees that may have first sent roots into the soil more than one hundred years ago. Biotic components also include every animal, large or small, that lives in the ecosystem.

Abiotic components include sunlight, water, air, and soil nutrients. The amount of rainfall, the changes in temperature, natural fires that may sweep through an area—these are all

Ecologists

Ecologists are scientists who study the relationships between organisms and their environment. Ecology blends several sciences such as biology, chemistry, physics—even computer science. Ecologists study environments of all types—air, land, and sea. They rely on scientists who study geology, climate, and oceans to help them understand changes in the different environments. People are beginning to recognize how tightly connected we are to the world around us. Ecologists help make the importance of those connections even clearer.

▲ A polar bear's white fur helps it blend in with its icy environment. The bear's coloring helps it hunt swimming seals that might not see it.

abiotic components of ecosystems. The abiotic parts of an ecosystem help determine the kinds of animals and plants that live within the ecosystem. An animal with very little fur would not live in an ecosystem where snow and ice are the most common features. A plant that has thin, feathery leaves that easily dry out would not be found in a parched desert ecosystem.

Interactions and Connections

Because the biotic and abiotic parts are always interacting, they shape, or affect, each other. Imagine a large, grassy field. The plants in the field anchor the soil. Worms and beetles are busy moving around in the soil, loosening it. This makes it easier for larger burrowing animals such as gophers or moles to create the tunnels and underground pockets in which they live. The tunnels create mounds in the field. The mounds, in turn, affect how the water flows through the field when it rains. Water flows differently on a hilly surface than on a flat surface.

An ecosystem's biotic parts also interact with each other. A roving bee pollinates a flower. Animals such as rabbits or caterpillars eat plants. Other, larger animals eat the rabbits and mice. Worms in the soil eat dead organic matter. Squirrels in an oak tree scatter acorns. Everything in an ecosystem is connected in some way.

The interactions between organisms and their physical environment also control the number of organisms that exist on Earth and where they live. Each organism is a member of several connected systems.

Individuals

An ecosystem includes plants and animals. A pond ecosystem might have minnows, turtles, and water lilies. Water strider insects may zip along a pond's surface while a dragonfly hovers nearby. It is likely that kingfisher birds live around this pond, as do larger animals, such as raccoons. By itself, each of these plants and animals is an individual

within the ecosystem. One dragonfly, one water lily, or one kingfisher is each an example of an individual.

▲ A single Gaudy leaf tree frog is an individual within its ecosystem.

Populations

A group of individuals of the same species living together in an ecosystem is called a population. All the water lilies on

▲ A flock of migrating geese is an example of a population.

the pond form a population. So do all the minnows. All the kingfishers that live in the pond ecosystem also form a population. A population can be as small as a pair of nesting waterbirds or as large as thousands of mosquitoes.

Communities

A community includes all the populations that live in the same area and that interact with each other. Like an ecosystem, a community can be very small or very large. A pond is an example of a fairly small community. Smoky Mountain National Park is an example of a very large community.

The populations within a community provide each other with food or shelter—sometimes both. In the pond community, the water lily population provides food for ducks that visit the pond. The plants also provide shade for fish swimming in the water. The fish provide food for the raccoons. The water in the pond is used by plants and animals alike. The populations in the pond community depend on each other to live.

Relationships within Ecosystems

The relationships between the populations in a community hold the community together. These relationships

In a community, the populations of plants and animals interact with each other.

are always changing. If the pond is located in an area that has seasonal changes, there will be more plants in the summer. The weather is warmer; there is more sunshine; it is a good time of year for plants to grow. During that season, certain insects come into the community because they depend on the plants for food and shelter. More plants mean more insects. Because insects are a food source for many pond animals, there will also be more of those animals during the summer season.

With the arrival of winter, there is less sunlight, and the temperatures are colder. The changes in these abiotic components affect plant growth. The organisms that depend on plants for food or shelter will temporarily leave the community. Insects may die off. Other animals may temporarily move, or migrate, to another community in search of food and shelter. Most people have heard of some birds "flying south" for the winter. This is an example of populations reacting to seasonal changes in their community.

Habitat

In any community or ecosystem, each population lives in an area called a habitat. The habitat supplies the population with everything it needs to survive: food, water, shelter, and space. The kingfisher's habitat includes shelter in the form of a tunnel and chamber the bird has dug into the steep banks of a pond or river. This shelter provides protection from weather and other animals that might be thinking about a lunch of kingfisher eggs. The kingfisher's habitat also provides it with food in the form of small fish in the pond and a variety of insects.

Niches

Two or more populations with similar needs may share a habitat. For example, the shallow water along the banks of the pond may also be home to cattail plants that thrive in the wet soil. Amoebas are

▲ A kingfisher finds a meal in a nearby pond. Its habitat provides the kingfisher with food, water, shelter, and space.

single-celled organisms that live in many environments, including ponds. Even though cattails, kingfishers, and amoebas share the same habitat, each population has a different role, or job. The specific role an organism plays within an ecosystem is called its niche. An organism's niche includes all the activities and behaviors that the organism needs to survive. The niche describes how the organism interacts with all of the biotic and abiotic parts of the ecosystem. How does the organism get its food? What does it do to find shelter?

Looking at the pond ecosystem, the amoeba and the kingfisher have different niches. The kingfisher builds a nest and eats fish and insects. The pond amoeba does not build a nest of any kind and eats bacteria, plant cells, and algae. The cattails, of course, don't nest either, but they get what they need from the pond water, soil, and sunlight. The cattails' niche is to provide food and shelter for other pond populations.

Broad Niches

Organisms within ecosystems can have either broad or narrow niches. Organisms with broad niches are able to live in a variety of places. They are able to eat many types of food. A raccoon is an example of an organism with a very broad niche. Raccoons eat everything from nuts and berries to frogs and dragonfly larvae. They can live in abandoned burrows, tree hollows, or caves. Other broad-niche organisms include cockroaches, mice, coyotes, and people.

Narrow Niches

Organisms that have narrow niches can survive only in a particular habitat. Often they can eat only a few types of foods. The giant pandas of China are good examples of organisms with a very narrow niche. They eat little other than bamboo, so they must live where there are plentiful supplies of that food. Bamboo does not grow in many places. Therefore, giant pandas don't live in many places either.

Ecosystem Diversity

Some ecosystems support a wide variety of plant and animal life. Other ecosystems have far less of a variety. Diversity refers to the number of different kinds of organisms that live within an ecosystem. Why is one ecosystem's diversity different from another's? Diversity depends on the ecosystem's ability to meet the needs of the organisms that live there. That ability is based in large part on where the ecosystem is located. Ecosystems close to the equator usually have a greater variety of species than ecosystems close to the North and South Poles. Think about year-round warmth and a lot of water compared with year-round subzero temperatures and all the water in the form of ice! If you were a green, leafy plant, where would you prefer to live?

Many of the ecosystems close to the equator are tropical rain forests. Some scientists estimate that about 50 percent of the world's animal and plant species are located in these ecosystems. That makes tropical rain-forest ecosystems the most diverse in the world. As with all other ecosystems, the populations in the tropical rain forest depend on the ecosystem to provide them with food, water, and shelter. If something happens that prevents the ecosystem from meeting their needs, the populations will decrease.

Ecosystems form strong connections between their abiotic components and their populations and communities. Even what seem to be small changes in an ecosystem can have far-reaching effects. For example, a rain forest can have one hundred different types of trees living on 2.5 acres (1 hectare) of land. Suppose someone decides that removing all the trees from that land would make it good for farming. The land might be useful for farming, but removing those trees would also affect all the other organisms that depend on the trees for food or shelter. Remove enough trees and the entire ecosystem could be put in danger.

Gambling with the Rain Forest

The rain forest is already a source of medicines to fight diseases, including malaria. The rain forest provides food products, such as bananas, coffee, and cocoa. There are many species of plants and animals in rain forests that have not yet been discovered. Which of those organisms might be the source of an important new medicine? What new plant might exist that could help to feed the world's people? These things need to be considered when actions are taken that change the rain-forest ecosystem. All types of ecosystems have secrets yet to be discovered. It is important to protect all the world's ecosystems so that those secrets are not lost.

3 ECOSYSTEM ENERGY FLOW

Organisms in ecosystems need energy for every part of life. Breathing, digesting food, moving around—these are all very basic activities. Basic or not, they all require some type of energy. Organisms get this energy from food. Some organisms, producers, are able to make their own food using a process called photosynthesis. Examples of producers include green plants, algae, lichens, mosses, and phytoplankton.

Energy from Sunlight

During photosynthesis, producers use the energy in sunlight, plus water and carbon dioxide, to manufacture sugars that the producers use for food. They also release oxygen into the atmosphere. Producing oxygen is beneficial because all living things need oxygen to breathe; so producers and photosynthesis are central to the health of our planet. Photosynthesis not only produces the oxygen other organisms need to breathe, the process also uses parts of carbon dioxide gas. Carbon dioxide is basically a waste

product of breathing. So, one part of photosynthesis gives us one of the things we need to live while another part of the process reuses some of the waste.

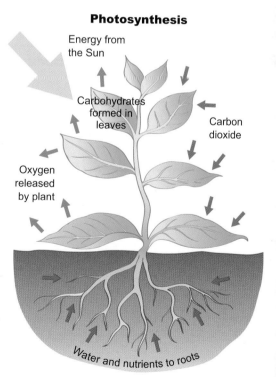

Photosynthesis

Energy from the Sun

Carbohydrates formed in leaves

Carbon dioxide

Oxygen released by plant

Water and nutrients to roots

▲ During photosynthesis, producers like this plant use water, carbon dioxide, and energy from the Sun to make their own food. Photosynthesis also produces the oxygen most living things need to breathe.

Chemosynthesis

Sunlight cannot reach all places on Earth. Deep in the world's oceans there are producers that use a special process called chemosynthesis to make their own food. Chimneylike vents called hydrothermal vents are found at mid-ocean ridges on the ocean floor. These vents emit some chemicals that certain types of bacteria use to produce their own food. Like cyanobacteria and green plants, the deep-sea producers also store food in their bodies to use later.

Carbon Fixation

Carbon fixation is an important part of the photosynthetic process. Carbon atoms are taken from the carbon dioxide molecules in the atmosphere and converted to other chemicals. These eventually become the food sugar that producers need. While oxygen is what we need to breathe, carbon dioxide is what we exhale. During photosynthesis, producers cycle this gas and use it to make their own food while also manufacturing something that almost every living thing on Earth needs—oxygen.

Most producers are green plants, but there are certain bacteria called cyanobacteria that are also able to make their own food. Cyanobacteria are usually single-celled organisms that live in water. Like plants, they use photosynthesis to manufacture sugars for food and release oxygen into the atmosphere. Cyanobacteria have been part of ecosystems for more than 3.5 billion years, long before plants came into existence. In fact, scientists believe that cyanobacteria were responsible for helping to create Earth's oxygen-rich atmosphere.

The food that producers make for themselves is not all used right away. Some of the food is stored in the roots, stems, and leaves of the plant or in the cells of photosynthetic bacteria. This is good news for consumers of plants and other producers. These consumers are organisms that cannot make their own food. They get their food energy by eating other organisms.

Different Consumers

Within an ecosystem, there are different types of consumers. Consumers that eat only producers are called herbivores. Rabbits, deer, and almost all caterpillars are examples of herbivores. Green sea turtles and manatees are examples of herbivores in an ocean ecosystem. Consumers that eat only other consumers are carnivores. Mountain lions, alligators,

▲ Vultures are examples of special consumers called scavengers. They eat the dead animal and plant remains left behind by other consumers.

spiders, and great white sharks are examples of carnivores. An omnivore is an organism that eats both producers and other consumers. Bears, raccoons, bearded dragon lizards, and wasps are examples of omnivores. Human beings are omnivores, too, but they may choose not to eat parts of an omnivore diet.

There are two special groups of consumers: scavengers and decomposers. Scavengers eat only the remains of dead animals and plants. One of the most easily recognizable scavengers is the vulture. Vultures feed on animals that have died. If a lion kills a zebra and leaves some of the meat behind, vultures will arrive to finish off the meal. Seagulls and crows

also scavenge if the opportunity arises. Crows often scavenge animals that have been killed along roadsides. Cockroaches are very efficient scavengers. They see a huge variety of producer and consumer material as food. In a freshwater ecosystem, there are animals called tubifex worms that bury their heads in the bottom of a pond and eat dead plants.

Decomposers are an ecosystem's "clean-up crew." Without decomposers, Earth would be crowded with piles of animal and plant remains. Perhaps, you've seen a rotting log in a forest. If you look closely, you'll probably see unusual mushrooms attached to the log. These mushrooms are fungi that help break down the wood fibers. Earthworms, fungi, bacteria, and other microorganisms are common types of decomposers.

Decomposers eat dead animal and plant material. They break down the organic matter and return nutrients to the soil or water. Decomposers are very important members of any ecosystem food chain, yet they are often overlooked. In the case of the pond food chain, there is sure to be dead plant or animal material left behind in the water. A single-celled organism such as a paramecium would feed on this material, breaking it down into nutrients that would enter the water.

▲ Mushrooms are decomposers that break down organic material such as this fallen log. The mushrooms get the nutrients they need while also returning nutrients to the soil.

Food Chains

In all ecosystems, energy is passed from organism to organism in food chains and food webs. A food chain is the path of food energy through a sequence of producers and consumers. A food chain represents a single path of how food energy is transferred from organism to organism. A food chain always begins with a producer and the energy it has stored.

When a consumer eats a producer, some of the energy stored in the producer passes to the consumer. If another consumer comes along and eats the first consumer, some of the energy in the first consumer passes to the second consumer. In this way, all organisms in an ecosystem get the energy they need to live. In a pond ecosystem, a typical food chain might include green algae that are eaten by a tadpole. The tadpole is eaten by a crayfish (crawdad). Then a raccoon comes along and eats the crayfish. Starting with the producer, the algae, energy is passed on through each consumer in the food chain. Decomposers are also a part of the food chain. Even animal and plant waste has food energy in it. Decomposers break down this waste at each stage of the food chain, returning food nutrients to the soil or water.

Food Webs

A food web is a group of interconnected food chains. While a food chain represents a single path of food energy transfer, a food web represents several paths. A food web connects food chains in many ways.

In most ecosystems, organisms consume more than one type of food. Algae may be food for pond snails and fish. In turn, the pond snails may be food for mice and wild ducks. The mice may be food for foxes, raccoons, and hawks. The foxes and raccoons may also eat the fish.

Pond Food Web

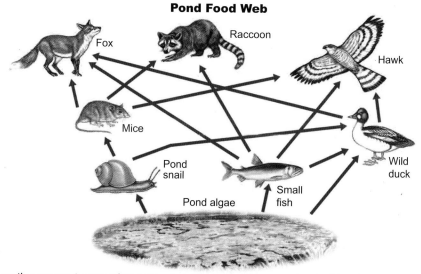

▲ Follow the arrows to see what eats what. Decomposers operate at all levels of the food web breaking down waste, such as dead plants and animals, into nutrients for the soil or water.

Poison Webs

As each animal in a food web feeds, energy is passed from consumer to consumer. Along with energy, poisons or toxins can be passed from organism to organism. Toxins stay in the body of an organism that absorbs or eats them. If this organism is eaten in turn, it passes the toxins up through the food chain. The animal at the top of the food chain or web gets all the toxins that may be present in each level of the food chain. This process is called biomagnification. The toxins may come from pesticides meant to control harmful organisms. Other toxins come from industrial waste. Because human beings are often at the top of most food webs, biomagnification piles up the toxins and poses a real hazard for people.

Energy Pyramids

In all ecosystems, organisms use food energy in similar ways. When a rabbit eats grass, it uses some of the energy stored in the grass. The rabbit also loses some of that energy as heat as it moves around. The rest of the energy from the grass is stored in the rabbit's body. A fox spots the rabbit and eats it. The same thing happens. Some energy is used, some is lost as heat, some is stored. A mountain lion now eats the fox. Once again, some energy is used, some is lost as heat, and some is stored. At each stage of the food chain, more and more of the energy stored in the grass is lost.

An energy pyramid shows how much energy is passed along from organism to organism in a food chain.

Different Level Consumers

Producers make up the base of the energy pyramid. The next level is the first-level consumers. These are the herbivores that eat the producers. Second-level consumers are the next group up in the energy pyramid. They eat the first-level consumers. Third-level consumers are next. They eat the second-level consumers. Each level going up an energy pyramid gets smaller and smaller because less food energy is being

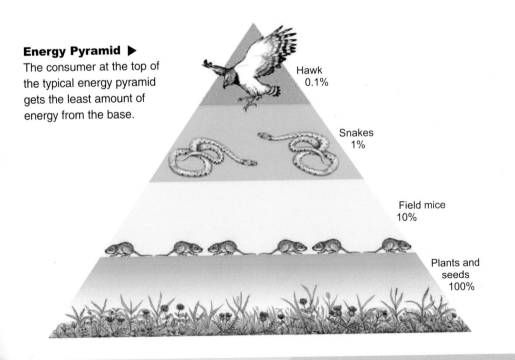

Energy Pyramid ▶
The consumer at the top of the typical energy pyramid gets the least amount of energy from the base.

Hawk
0.1%

Snakes
1%

Field mice
10%

Plants and
seeds
100%

passed up. At each level, only about 10 percent of the energy is transferred to the level above.

Consumers do not necessarily stay at one level or another at all times. This is especially true for omnivores. For example, when a bear eats berries, it is acting as a first-level consumer, just like any other herbivore. If the bear eats a rabbit, however, it becomes a second-level consumer.

Energy pyramids explain how populations are distributed in ecosystems. In most cases, producers have the largest populations because they make their own food. This means they have the most energy available to them. Even so, remember that only 10 percent of the energy stored in producers passes up to the first-level consumer. Because there is less energy available, there are fewer first-level consumers than producers. First-level consumers need to eat a lot of producers to get the energy they need.

There are even fewer second-level consumers than first-level consumers. Again, energy is lost as you move up the food pyramid. This means that to get enough food energy, second-level consumers have to eat large numbers of first-level consumers. Because of this, second-level consumers may need to travel over larger areas within the ecosystem. The higher an organism's level on the energy pyramid, the larger the area in the ecosystem it will need to find enough food energy to survive. The animals at the top of the energy pyramid

Choosing Your Place in the Energy Pyramid

Unlike other animals in an ecosystem, human beings can choose what level consumer they will be. Because we are omnivores, we can survive on plants or animals or both. Since you can choose what kind of consumer you will be, you might want to think about which level of consumer uses the Sun's energy most efficiently. You really like steak, so you want to be a second-level consumer and eat only meat. You would probably need the meat from about 10 cattle to keep yourself in steak. The cattle, however, need to eat so you'll probably need about 5 acres (2 ha) of grass for them. Now, if you decided to be a first-level consumer and eat only wheat, you'd only need about 1 acre (0.4 ha) of land. Being a first-level consumer uses the Sun's energy more efficiently because more food for people can be grown per acre of land than food for livestock, which is then used as food for people. Sometimes, choosing to be a first-level consumer is a wise choice.

have to cover even more area to find food. Lions, hawks, and killer whales have large hunting areas. Most ecosystems can support only a few different populations of third-level consumers. As you go up the energy pyramid, there are fewer populations of consumers.

Competing for Resources

In ecosystems, the populations of different organisms all need some light, space, water, food, and shelter. The ecosystems should provide the resources to meet these needs. Some of these resources, such as food, shelter, space, and water, may be limited. When two or more species need the same limited resource, the result is competition for that resource.

There are several different types of competition within ecosystems. In one type, one species may do something to prevent another species from using a resource. Sagebrush plants release a chemical into the soil that prevents some other plant species from growing close to it. The sagebrush lives in an ecosystem where the soil is very dry and water is scarce. The chemicals it releases are the sagebrush's way of competing for these two limited resources.

As the human population grows, there is more and more competition for open space. People want the space to build towns and cities. However, the wildlife in an area needs the space for shelter, food, and water. In most cases, people win the battle for space because they are more powerful than wildlife.

▲ As third-level consumers, killer whales have to travel over a wide area of ocean to get enough food to survive.

▲ This part of Brazil was once all rain forest. Clearing the rain forest for human occupation has increased the competition between humans and wildlife for space.

Reducing Competition

One way of reducing competition for a particular resource is to inhabit separate niches. A type of bird called a warbler lives in evergreen forests. There may be five different species of warblers living and hunting in the same trees within the forest. They also all eat the same food—insects. The warblers solve the problem of competing for insect resources by looking for those insects in different parts of the tree. Two warbler species look in the top section of trees. Two other species hunt in different parts of the middle section of trees. One species hunts only in the lowest section of trees. Each species fills a particular niche. All the species share the same resource, but not in the same exact place.

Tied Together for Survival

Predator/prey relationships limit the populations of both the predator and its prey. These types of relationships help maintain balance in an ecosystem. Predators obtain food by killing and eating other animals. The animals eaten by a predator are called prey. In the photo above, a lion is the predator and a kudu is the prey. Predators actually help prey animals because predators tend to capture prey animals that are weak or sick. Removing weak animals from a population allows only the stronger members to survive and reproduce. At the same time, limiting the numbers of prey populations also limits the population of the predator. If too many prey are killed, the predators starve. They do not reproduce, and their numbers fall. When the predators' numbers decrease, the prey numbers start to go up again. Once more, plentiful prey means the predators' population can also rise. Predators and prey are tied together in this continous struggle for survival.

Symbiosis among Organisms

Beside the predator/prey relationship, organisms within an ecosystem can have another type of relationship. The relationship is called symbiosis, and it describes a close living relationship between two different species. Symbiosis often results in some very odd relationships. The three types of symbiotic relationships between organisms are mutualism, commensalism, and parasitism.

Mutualism

Mutualism describes a relationship in which both species benefit. It can represent some pretty unusual partnerships. One example is the relationship between giant moray eels and tiny rock shrimps. Moray eels live in coral or rocky reefs. Some of these eels can reach lengths of 5 feet (1.5 meters) to 8 feet (2.4 m). They also have mouths full of very sharp, needlelike teeth. Despite their scary appearance, they often share their homes with shrimps that may be only a few inches long. The shrimps pluck and eat tiny organisms that have attached themselves to the eel. The shrimps even crawl around the eel's sharp teeth, cleaning them by removing particles of food. In return for this all-over cleaning service, the eels don't eat the shrimps. Both organisms benefit.

Commensalism

Commensalism describes a relationship in which one organism benefits and the other organism is neither helped nor harmed. In tropical rain forests, certain types of orchids attach themselves to branches of trees. In this location, the orchid gets more sunlight. The tree, on the other hand, is not affected at all. In an ocean ecosystem, small remora fish attach themselves to cruising sharks, turtles, and whales. The remoras get a ride to better feeding areas without using too much of their own energy. Sometimes they get the leftovers from their host's meal as well.

▲ Mutualism exists between this gold-spotted eel and tiny shrimps. Both species benefit.

Parasitism

Parasitism is a symbiotic relationship in which one organism benefits and the other is harmed. In most cases, the organism that benefits—the parasite—lives on or in another organism—the host. Ticks are very common parasites that attach themselves to a wide variety of organisms. A tick burrows its head beneath its host's skin and feeds on the host's blood. Even though the tick does not take enough blood to kill its host, it may carry diseases that can seriously harm the host. Lyme disease, which affects both animals and people, is carried by ticks. Plants can have parasites, too. The famous Christmas plant, mistletoe, is a parasite that grows on oak and other types of trees. The mistletoe's roots reach into the branches of the host tree, absorbing the tree's nutrients. Without the nutrients it needs, the tree is often weakened. If enough mistletoe is present, the tree can die.

▲ Mistletoe grows in clumps on the trunk and branches of a host tree. This parasitic relationship may eventually kill the tree.

You're Never Alone!

The human body has entire ecosystems living within it. Take your large intestines, for example. A large number of bacteria live in your intestines. Some bacteria live off your undigested food and produce vitamin K, which is needed for blood clotting. This is an example of mutualism. In that same intestinal ecosystem, however, there can be examples of parasitism as well. A disease called cholera is caused by bacteria that enter the body through contaminated food or water. Once in your system, these bacteria will be healthy and happy, but you won't be feeling well at all. Cholera causes intense vomiting and severe diarrhea and, if not treated, can result in death. Cholera remains a serious health threat in countries with contaminated water supplies.

4 NATURAL CYCLES

Earth has a series of natural cycles that work to keep the biotic and abiotic components of ecosystems interacting in a balanced way. The change from day to night and the changing of the tides are cycles that are easily noticed. Other cycles are not as visible but are so important that life could not exist without them. All of the organisms on Earth need certain materials to live and grow. Some of these materials pass through natural cycles in which they are used and reused over and over again.

The Water Cycle

No matter where an ecosystem is located, the organisms that live in it need water. Water moves continuously throughout Earth in a water cycle. The water molecules that hit your face in the form of rain may once have been part of the Nile River in Egypt. The water you drink might have once existed as part of an Antarctic iceberg at the South Pole.

Water molecules constantly move from Earth to the atmosphere and back again in a three-stage cycle. The Sun's energy changes water from a liquid to a gas in a process called evaporation. Water in its gaseous state is called water vapor. Water evaporates from oceans, rivers, lakes, soil, and even the bodies of animals. Once water evaporates, it is held in Earth's atmosphere as water

▲ Precipitation returns water to Earth as part of the water cycle.

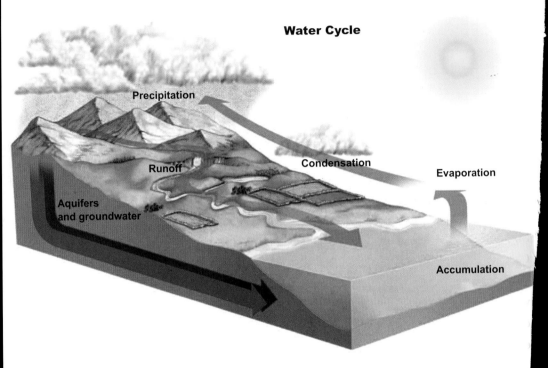

Water Cycle

Precipitation

Runoff

Condensation

Evaporation

Aquifers and groundwater

Accumulation

▲ The water cycle is a continuous process of evaporation, condensation, precipitation, and accumulation. This cycle produces enough liquid water to support life on Earth.

vapor. The amount of water vapor the atmosphere can hold depends on the air temperature. If you've experienced a particularly hot, humid day, you have felt water vapor on your skin and clothes.

As the air temperature cools, water vapor once again becomes liquid through the condensation process. Condensed water forms fog, steam, and clouds. Eventually, the condensed water falls back to Earth as precipitation. Rain, sleet, snow, and hail are forms of precipitation. Most of the water that

How Do Plants and Animals Cycle Water?

Plants and animals also interact with the atmosphere to cycle water. Plants use water from the ground for their life processes and release some of that water back into the air. Animals also use water for their life processes. Some of that water is returned to the atmosphere when animals exhale as they breathe.

vaporizes and condenses to form precipitation comes from Earth's oceans. Most precipitation, however, falls over land. This is because the clouds that form over the oceans drift over land. Precipitation that falls on dry soil may become part of the water held in soil—which is called groundwater. This water may be close to the surface or may move farther down into the soil. Some of this water is used by plants. Groundwater might also bubble up somewhere as a forest spring. Once water reaches Earth's surface, the water cycle begins again when the water evaporates and condenses.

The Carbon Cycle

Carbon is a part of every organism on Earth. It is in your DNA and in compounds such as sugars, carbohydrates, and proteins. Earth's crust contains carbon in the forms of coal, oil, and natural gas. Despite carbon's importance, it is in limited supply. The carbon never runs out, however, because it is reused in the carbon cycle.

The carbon cycle describes the movement of carbon through Earth's ecosystems. Carbon moves through as a solid, a liquid, or a gas. It moves through the carbon cycle most commonly as carbon dioxide (CO_2) gas.

As part of the carbon cycle, these plants use carbon dioxide gas to make food.

Carbon enters the biotic parts of ecosystems through plants and other photosynthetic organisms such as cyanobacteria. During the process of photosynthesis, carbon as CO_2 gas is used by these producers to make the sugars they need for food. Some of this food is stored as a starch.

The process of using the stored energy from photosynthesis begins when a consumer eats a plant. The consumer's digestive systems break down the plant tissue to get the stored starch. The sugars and other nutrients in the starch travel to the consumer's cells. As the consumer breathes, it takes in oxygen. The oxygen releases the energy in the sugars and nutrients. CO_2 is produced while this is happening. The CO_2 is released into the air. Decomposers are consumers and also play an important part in the carbon cycle. When they break down dead animal and plant matter to get food, they also release carbon dioxide.

Human Activity and the Carbon Cycle

About two hundred years ago, many countries entered the Industrial Age. Manufacturing processes such as weaving and furniture-making went from

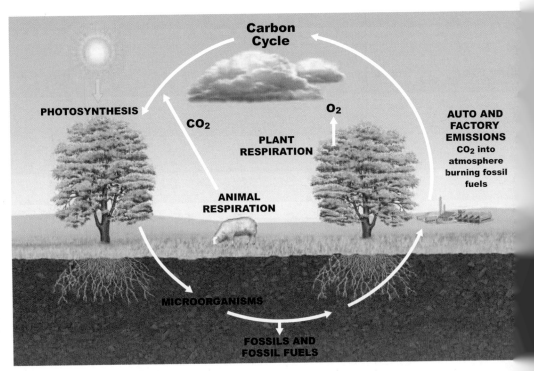

individuals using hand tools or looms to machinery driven by a variety of engines. The engines needed energy to run. That energy came from large amounts of coal, oil, and gas. Burning these materials released fossilized carbon in the form of carbon dioxide into the atmosphere and into the carbon cycle.

Since that time, the world's population has grown. Larger and larger cities mean more and more fuel being burned in factories, homes, and vehicles. Greater amounts of carbon dioxide are being released into the atmosphere. Forests have also been burned to clear land for agriculture and other development. Burning wood releases carbon dioxide into the atmosphere. Natural carbon cycles are only able to recycle a certain amount of carbon. Human activity is overloading the carbon cycle system with the result that there is more carbon dioxide in the atmosphere than there should be.

Greenhouse Effect

Carbon dioxide in the atmosphere helps to trap the sun's heat. This process is called the greenhouse effect. Increased temperatures are causing major changes in Earth's ecosystems. Warmer temperatures in the northern regions are causing

▲ As the world's population increases, so does the number of vehicles. Each vehicle produces harmful carbon dioxide that affects the balance of the carbon cycle.

Living in a Greenhouse

If you've ever visited a botanical garden or a farmer's market, you may have stood inside a greenhouse. A greenhouse is a building with glass walls that let in the Sun's light. Once inside, the sunlight becomes heat. The glass walls prevent the heat from escaping, so it warms the plants inside the greenhouse. This is how the greenhouse effect got its name. It describes how, like glass greenhouse walls, carbon dioxide helps trap heat in Earth's atmosphere.

polar ice caps to melt. This causes the ocean levels to rise and move farther inland. Warmer temperatures have also resulted in hot, dry summers that have damaged wheat and corn as well as other crops around the world. The simplest way to reduce the greenhouse effect is to burn less fossil fuel and forest.

The Nitrogen Cycle

Like carbon, nitrogen cycles through Earth's ecosystems. About 78 percent of Earth's atmosphere is made up of nitrogen gas. The abundance of nitrogen is a real benefit to organisms because plants and animals need nitrogen to make proteins. Even though there is a lot of available nitrogen, most organisms can't use nitrogen gas taken straigh from the air. The nitrogen must be changed into a form that plants can use. This change of form in the nitrogen cycl is called nitrogen fixation.

Bacteria that live in soil or water can fix, or change, the nitrogen in nitrogen gas. These bacteria grow on the roots of certain plants, such as soybeans, peanuts, peas, and beans. The bacteria on these plants help nitrogen gas change into nitrogen compounds. The compounds are materials that plants can absorb to make proteins. When an animal eats a plant, it gets the nitrogen from the plant proteins. The proteins and nitrogen

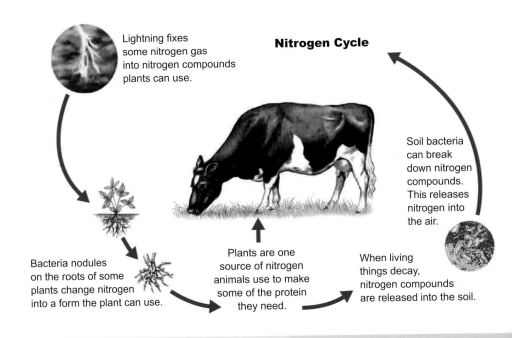

Nitrogen Cycle

Lightning fixes some nitrogen gas into nitrogen compounds plants can use.

Soil bacteria can break down nitrogen compounds. This releases nitrogen into the air.

Bacteria nodules on the roots of some plants change nitrogen into a form the plant can use.

Plants are one source of nitrogen animals use to make some of the protein they need.

When living things decay, nitrogen compounds are released into the soil.

are passed along the food chain as animal eats animal. Eventually, plants and animals die. When they do, decomposers break down the nitrogen compounds in the dead matter and release nitrogen gas back into the air. Once in the air, the nitrogen gas enters the nitrogen cycle once again.

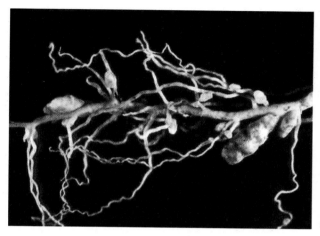

▲ These are nitrogen-fixing nodules on clover roots. Bacteria change the nitrogen into nitrogen compounds that the plants can absorb.

Human Activity and the Nitrogen Cycle

Because nitrogen is of such great benefit to plants and animals, it only makes sense that nitrogen would be a great plant fertilizer. It is. Nitrogen is the main ingredient in many fertilizers. Farmers use nitrogen-rich fertilizers in soil to help their crops grow; when the crops are harvested, the nitrogen goes with them. Irrigation and erosion also pull nitrogen out of the soil. Nitrogen must be returned to the soil so that other crops can grow, so farmers use more fertilizer.

Using nitrogen fertilizers, however, can also cause problems in an ecosystem. Rain can wash the nitrogen off the fields and into natural water sources such as lakes and rivers. The nitrogen compounds in the water cause too much algae to grow. The algae die, and decomposers move in. When they do, they use up too much of the water's oxygen. A loss of oxygen kills fish and other water organisms.

Lightning Strikes!

The next time you see bolts of lightning crackling through the sky, think about how they are benefiting all of us! The energy released by lightning combines nitrogen gas and the oxygen in the air. Rain and snow carry the nitrogen compounds to the ground. As the soil absorbs the water, plants absorb the nitrogen. The plant grows and passes the nitrogen on to other organisms that eat the plants.

Integrated Pest Management

There is little doubt that most chemical pesticides hurt more than just the pests they are designed to kill. At the same time, farmers around the world cannot afford to lose large portions of their crops to pests. One idea that is gaining popularity is called integrated pest management, or IPM. With this approach, pests are controlled through the use of a combination of methods that do not pose a danger to an ecosystem. Aphids are small insects that cause major problems in many types of vegetable crops. In the past, toxic chemicals were used to kill the aphids before they killed the crops.

With IPM, a natural predator of the aphids, such as a particular type of wasp, is released into the crop areas. The wasp doesn't harm people or crops but helps control the aphid population. The wasp is considered a beneficial insect because of the service it performs. This same crop area might also use a type of vacuum device to suck aphids and other pests off the crops without damaging the vegeation. These two methods, combined with the planting of the most disease-resistant crop in the first place, can help protect the crop without an ecosystem paying the price.

Succession

Ecosystems go through cycles of change called succession. During these cycles, the types of communities in the ecosystem change over a long period of time. A certain type of plant species may exist in an area for thousands of years. As the environment changes, that plant species may gradually die out and be replaced by a different species.

Primary Succession

There are two types of succession, primary and secondary. In primary succession, plants begin to grow where there were no plants before. A dramatic event such as a volcanic eruption could destroy all plant and animal life in a specific area. At some point, the eruption will end, and the lava will cool. The process of primary succession begins when the first plants begin to push through the barren lava rock.

▲ Plants growing through hardened lava on Mount St. Helens, Washington, are an examp of primary succession.

Secondary Succession

A secondary succession cycle begins when most, but not all, of the plants in an area are removed. A wildfire might sweep through a forest and seem to destroy everything in its path. In the soil, however, there may remain some plants that have escaped the blaze. Even if it seems as if every tree and bush in the forest has been destroyed, plant life soon begins to come back. Grasses and weeds grow. Next, hardy shrubs start to grow. Over time, trees begin to reappear. Pines and other fast-growing trees are usually the first to come back. Hardwood trees, such as oak and ash, grow more slowly, but over time they, too, start to root. It might take more than one hundred years, but the forest eventually returns.

▲ This area of forest in Montana's Glacier National Park shows secondary succession after a forest fire has stripped the trees of their leaves.

Succession on Mount St. Helens

On May 18, 1980, a volcano in Washington state erupted with enough force to peel off the top 1,300 feet (400 m) of the mountain. The blast was so powerful, it forced all the water out of one of the mountain lakes. A flow of burning lava and ash killed every living thing in its path. It seemed impossible that anything could ever grow again on the mountain. After two years, a plant with tiny purple flowers began to grow through the hard, dry surface. The plant had sprouted from a prairie lupine seed that had been washed down the mountainside. The lupines were able to fix nitrogen from the air and use it to help the plants grow. As the plants died off, they decomposed and added nitrogen to the thin layer of soil that was forming. Now, years after the huge eruption, the lupine has been mainly replaced by other plants. The lake is full of clear water in which fat trout swim. The cycle of succession is on daily display on Mount St. Helens.

5 WORLD BIOMES

Earth has a number of connected ecosystems called biomes. Biomes cover large areas of Earth. They are defined by the type of climate each biome has and the types of plants and animals that live there. Some biomes, such as those around the North and South Poles, or in high mountains, are very cold. These biomes support little life. Other biomes are just the opposite—hot and humid, with a great deal of rainfall. There are also biomes where the climate falls somewhere in between, with temperate climates. Earth includes nine major land biomes and two water biomes. The land biomes are polar, tundra, taiga, temperate forest, tropical rain forest, grasslands, chapparal/scrub, desert, and mountains. The water biomes are freshwater and ocean. These biomes exist in all parts of the world. For example, there are desert biomes in Africa, Australia, China, and North and South America.

Land Biomes

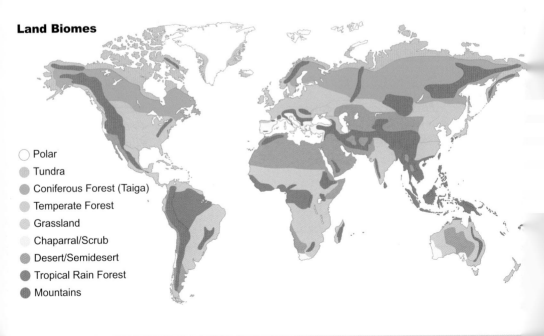

- Polar
- Tundra
- Coniferous Forest (Taiga)
- Temperate Forest
- Grassland
- Chaparral/Scrub
- Desert/Semidesert
- Tropical Rain Forest
- Mountains

What Affects a Biome's Climate?

The differences in biome climates can be classified by two main factors. One is the average amount of precipitation the biome receives in a year. The other factor is temperature. Precipitation describes the amount of moisture in the atmosphere that condenses to form rain, snow, sleet, and hail that then falls to Earth. Temperature describes the average warmth or cold a biome experiences over a certain period of time.

A biome's climate is most affected by its latitude. Climates close to the equator are warm and wet. The closer a biome is to one of the poles, the cooler and drier the biome is likely to be. There is less precipitation at the poles. In fact, the amount of precipitation received is as little as the driest desert! Whatever snow the poles do get doesn't melt. The water exists as ice and snow and evaporates very slowly over time.

Altitude also affects a biome's climate. Temperature drops as altitude increases. This is why some mountain peaks have snow on them all year round, even though they are located in a warm climate. The types of plants and animals that can live there are different from the organisms found toward the base of the mountain. The organisms that live in Earth's biomes have all developed physical traits that make it possible for them to live there.

Microclimates

Suppose you and your next-door neighbor planted small vegetable gardens. The gardens are exactly the same size, and you are growing the same vegetables. His vegetables, however, appear healthier than yours. Why? Even though only a few feet separate your houses, it might be a difference in microclimate. *Microclimate* means a "small climate." It reflects differences in environmental conditions in a limited area. Your vegetable garden may be just a few inches closer to your house, with the result that your vegetables spend more time in the shade than your neighbor's. Farmers use their knowledge of the microclimates in their crop fields to decide where to plant each specific crop. They try to plan crop types around even small differences in altitude to take advantage of differences in temperature and rainfall.

Rain-forest Biomes

What picture comes to your mind when someone says the word forest? Most likely, you think of trees. That is exactly what the main type of plant life is in a forest biome. The types of trees, though, vary depending on the biome's specific climate.

Rain forests get the most rain of any biome on Earth. Temperate rain forests are located along ocean coastlines such as the North American Pacific Northwest. These biomes get more than 100 inches (254 centimeters) of rain each year. Temperate rain forests have cooler temperatures than tropical rain forests which are located closer to the equator. This location means that the biome temperatures are very warm. Average temperatures range from about 64°F (18°C) to 95°F (35°C) all year round. Along with warm temperatures, tropical rain forests have an annual rainfall of as much as 400 inches (1,016 cm) of rain The leaves on many rain-forest plants are long with sharp or narrow tips. This shape makes it easier for water to run off the leaves.

In a rain-forest biome, the trees grow very tall and close together. Rain-forest

▲ Most toucans living in the wild probably spend their lives in rain-forest canopies.

Living in the Canopy

Some rain-forest animals live their entire lives in the dense leaves of the canopy. All of their needs for food, light, water, and shelter can be met among the vines and branches many feet above the forest floor. A pygmy marmoset is a type of monkey that rarely leaves its home in the canopy. All the insects, fruit, and tree sap it could ever want are easily within its reach. The marmoset shares its canopy home with birds and bats that find it as pleasant a place to live as the marmoset does.

ees grow so closely together that they rm a dense layer of leaves. The leaves retch like a high roof over the forest oor. The many species of plants in rain rests grow in layers. Plants that need e most sunlight grow toward the top of e forest's leafy "roof," which is called e canopy. Plants that need less sunlight actual shade grow closer to the forest oor. The concentration of so many ants in so large an area produces uch of the oxygen for the entire world.

The moisture and warmth of a tropi-l rain forest make it an ideal place to /e for many organisms. There is greater versity in tropical rain-forest biomes an in any other. More than 50 percent Earth's plant and animal species are cated in the tropical rain-forest biome. me scientists believe the number is oser to 90 percent. Many tropical rain-rest animals have brilliant colors and

unique features. The distinctive-looking toucan bird, with its oversized yellow beak has long been associated with tropical rain-forest jungles.

Temperate Forest Biomes

As with the rain-forest biomes, the temperate forest biome's main plants are trees. The temperate biome trees, however, are different. Temperate forests

▲ A temperate forest floor can be lush with vegetation. Fallen leaves produce good conditions for new growth.

have a greater range of temperatures that change along with four separate seasons. Throughout the year, temperatures can range from a very chilly -22°F (-30°C) to a very warm 86°F (30°C). The rainfall is only about half that of the rain forest biome, but it is still sufficient to support a variety of plant and animal life. The trees in the temperate forest biome are deciduous. This means that they lose their leaves in fall and remain leafless until spring.

The animals living in temperate forests are probably more familiar to most people than the exotic rain-forest creatures. Deer, bears, rabbits, squirrels, and skunks are well-known inhabitants.

Taiga Biomes

The taiga biome is another forest biome, but it couldn't be more different from the rain forest. The trees in the taiga are mainly conifers, which are trees with cones. Tall pines with thin, needle-like leaves are common taiga trees, as are the feathery-looking spruces and firs. The leaves on taiga biome trees are especially suited to life in a colder climate. Each short, waxy leaf helps keep in water.

The taiga has long, cold winters and short, cool summers. In the taiga, summer days where the temperature reaches even as high as 50°F (10°C) are few. The taiga also is much drier than the other forest biomes. It gets about 20 inches (50 cm) of precipitation, and most of that is snow. Most of the taiga biomes are located in the northern parts of North America and in northern Europe and Asia. Taller trees do not grow north of the taiga biome.

Animals such as moose, bears, wolves, and weasels call the taiga home. Birds such as owls and hawks also find the taiga comfortable. Despite the cold temperatures, insects such as mosquitoes and tiny midges can be found during the taiga summers.

▲ Moose are natural inhabitants of the taiga biome.

Grassland Biomes

The grassland biomes is the most common type of biome on Earth. Grasslands are found on every continent except Antarctica. The main feature of this biome is contained within its name—grass. Hundreds of different types of grasses grow in this biome. There are very few trees in a grassland biome because there is not enough rain to support tree growth. However, there is plenty of grass to make up for a lack of trees.

There are two types of grassland biomes: savannas and prairies. Imagine a lion hidden in a field of tall grass hungrily eyeing an unsuspecting zebra. This image is one many people think of when picturing savannas. Most savannas are found in warmer areas of the world, such as central Africa. In South America, a savanna biome is called the pampas. The savanna grassland biome can get as much as 40 inches (100 cm) of rain each year. The rain does not fall steadily throughout the year. Most savannas have a dry season, during which all but the smallest trees die off.

Elephants, giraffes, ostriches, and lions are examples of African savanna animals. Wild guinea pigs, maned wolves, and llamalike guanacos live in the South American savanna.

North America has miles of prairie grassland. Prairies are considered to be temperate climate areas, even though they can get very cold in the winter and very hot in the summer. Prairie temperatures can range from -40°F (-40°C) in the winter to 100°F (38°C) in the summer! In the United States, the prairie grassland

▲ African elephants roam the savanna searching for food and a water hole.

animals include hawks, coyotes, prairie dogs, salamanders, rattlesnakes, and meadowlarks.

Why Do Jumping Mice Jump?

Jumping mice are common grassland animals. Jumping mice are only about 3 to 4 inches (7.5 –10 cm) long, but they can jump as high as 13 feet (almost 4 meters) in one leap! These animals can live successfully in grasslands, even though the grasses are much taller than the mice. Being able to jump allows the mouse to take a quick look around for possible predators.

Chaparral/Scrub Biomes

A chaparral/scrub biome looks like a combination of prairie and desert. This biome is characterized by its hot and dry climate. Chaparral/scrub is usually found on the west coast of continents at latitudes of about 30° to 40° north and south of the equator. Summers are very hot with temperatures reaching 100°F (38°C). Winters are mild; temperatures drop to 50°F (10°C) only on the coolest days. The chaparral/scrub biome gets about 15 inches (38 cm) to 40 inches (100 cm) of rain each year. This is enough to support the low-growing scrub oak and sage that thrive in this biome. The animals that live in this biome are usually grassland animals that have adapted to a hotter and drier climate. Wild horses, coyotes, lizards, vultures, and eagles are examples of animals that find homes in the chaparral.

Desert Biomes

When people think of the desert, they often imagine rolling sand dunes and camels. While this image is correct, not all deserts look like that. There are four varieties of deserts: hot/dry, semi-arid, coastal, and cold. It is a common misconception that all deserts are hot. The one thing all deserts do have in common, though, is that they are the driest of all world biomes. Most deserts get less than 10 inches (25 cm) of rain each year. This amount may sound like quite a bit, but not if you spread it over an entire year. Most deserts get as little as one-fifth of an inch (.5 cm) of rain at a time. Some deserts don't get any rain at all.

Even though desert biomes are very dry, they are home to a greater variety of life than you might think. Like the organisms in all other biomes, desert plants and animals have characteristics

▲ This cactus wren finds a saguaro cactus a perfect place to build a nest.

that allow them to live in a dry environment. Some plants have thick, waxy stems that help store water. Their roots stretch outward many feet instead of reaching deep into the soil. This allows the roots to catch as much rainfall as possible before the water drains into the soil. Desert cacti are the best examples of these types of plants.

Along with dry conditions, deserts are usually very warm—at least during the day. Many desert biomes are found at latitudes about 20° or 30° north and south of the equator. Lizards, snakes, mice, spiders, and tortoises conserve energy by being fairly inactive during the hot part of the day and looking for food after the sun goes down. Staying quiet during the day also helps desert animals conserve water.

Tundra Biomes

The tundra biome sounds like a place where nothing could live. It is bitterly cold in the winter, with almost no rain at any time. It is so cold that the ground is almost always frozen. In some areas of the tundra, the ground stays frozen for hundreds of feet below the surface. During the brief summer months, the temperatures barely reach 50°F (10°C). In some areas, the ground thaws enough for plants such as mosses and lichens to grow. These plants grow low to the ground, which helps them survive cold winds and temperatures. Even though the tundra seems to be such an uninviting place, polar bears, reindeer, arctic foxes, and other animals have developed thick fur and body fat to help them live where it seems nothing could. Other animals, such as caribou, migrate to the tundra during the brief summer but move out during the harsh winter months.

Losing the Tundra

Increasing temperatures around the globe are making some of the tundra plants grow more than they ever have. Certain types of shrubs doubled in number in a short period of time. That might sound like a good thing, but it really is not. The growth of more trees on the tundra can upset the natural processes that cycle water and energy. This may result in the storage of too much carbon, threatening the balance of the ecosystem in the tundra biomes.

Ocean Biomes

Just as climate conditions define land biomes, there are similar features that describe water biomes. Oceans cover more than 70 percent of Earth's surface and are home to thousands of plant and animal species. Freshwater lakes, streams, and rivers have complete ecosystems of their own.

The ocean biome is divided into zones. The intertidal zone is the area that is covered and uncovered in the cycle of ocean tides. Sometimes this part of the ocean biome is under water; sometimes it is not. Because of this, the organisms that live in the intertidal zone have special characteristics that permit them to live in this regularly changing environment. The intertidal zone is home to a variety of crabs that can move over land or under water. Mollusks such as clams and mussels attach themselves to rocks so that they are not pulled out to sea when the tide goes out.

The near-shore zone is located just beyond the shoreline. This part of the biome is always under water. It is also home to an interesting variety of plants and animals. There is a type of underground forest that is made up of thick seaweed called kelp. Many kinds of fish live among the swaying kelp "trees," using the plants for shelter and for food. Animals that hunt the fish, such as otters, also swim in and out of the kelp.

Water is cold and deep in the third ocean biome zone. This one is called the open ocean zone. Sunlight can reach only

▲ Coral reefs are near-shore ecosystems found in ocean biomes. Coral reefs have some of the most diverse plants and wildlife in the sea.

bout 660 feet (200 m) into the ocean, so most of the ocean plants are located in his area. Algae float near the ocean urface and provide food for many of the cean biome's animals. Strange creatures ave developed in the darkest part of he ocean. Some are completely blind ecause there is no light by which to see. 'here are also fish that produce their wn light with special organs called hotophores or by a chemical reaction in heir bodies called bioluminescence. The ght is most often used to attract food.

Freshwater Biomes

Like the ocean biomes, freshwater systems have zones. Flowing water is a feature of streams and rivers. Moving water is considered to be one of the freshwater biome zones. Only fast-swimming fish, such as trout, could survive here. Salmon spawn in such streams as well. As the current slows downstream, it is easier for plants to take root. Where there are plants, of course, there are animals to eat them. Ducks, geese, and other waterfowl live in this zone, as do animals such as beavers and slower-moving fish.

Fresh, still bodies of water, such as deep ponds and lakes, have three zones. The first zone is the area near the surface of the pond or lake. This area is warmed by the sun and receives a great deal of light. These conditions make it a great place for plants, insects, microorganisms, and fish. Deeper into the water, it gets cooler. However, some light is still able to get through. Tiny organisms called plankton live in this middle zone. Plankton is a very important food for many freshwater fish. The third zone is the deepest and darkest part of the water and includes the pond or lake bottom. Here, bacteria and other decomposing organisms live. They help keep the water clean by breaking down dead plant and animal matter that sinks down through the other zones and winds up on the bottom.

▲ A bear stands at the top of a waterfall and gets ready to grab its next meal—a fast-swimming salm

6 KEEPING THE BALANCE

Earth's ecosystems and biomes represent a series of connections between all living and nonliving things. We have touched on examples of what happens if natural cycles are disturbed by either too much or too little involvement by the people who are also part of Earth's ecosystems and biomes.

For example, burning too many fossil fuels in our homes and vehicles floods Earth's atmosphere with carbon dioxide gas. This may lead to the greenhouse effect that seems to be causing an increase in temperatures all over the world. Warming temperatures can lead to losses in ecosystems and biomes. This is already happening with some of the tundra. As the tundra changes its character, it will also cause change in the organisms connected to that biome.

Everything on Earth is connected. Understanding those connections can help you be a better citizen of Earth. It can also help you see what role you play in the ecosystems and biomes of which you are a part.

You Can Make a Difference

He got really sick of seeing rotting tires and other junk hanging on the banks of the Mississippi River. It was an ugly sight; there must have been tons of the stuff all the way up and down one of the longest rivers in the United States.

What could one person do? As it turned out, one person could do a great deal. Chad Pregracke is a young man with a mission. In 1997, he and a few friends started to remove all the rusting metal, plastic containers, and other garbage that had been tossed into the Mississippi River for years. It must have seemed an impossible task. Using an old boat, he and his friends removed more and more garbage. In 1998, Chad founded a nonprofit environmental organization named Living Lands and Waters. Within a few years, Chad and his crews have removed more than 2 million tons of trash from the river. Living Lands and Waters now has a small fleet of barges and workboats and thousands of volunteers.

GLOSSARY

abiotic Nonliving components of an ecosystem, such as sunlight, water, air, and soil nutrients

amoeba Single-celled organism that lives in many environments, including ponds

bioluminescence A chemical reaction within the bodies of certain organisms that produce their own light

biome A large area of Earth that is defined by its type of climate and the types of plants and animals that live there

biotic Living components of an ecosystem including everything from microscopic bacteria to the largest trees and animals

carbon cycle The movement of carbon through Earth's ecosystems

carbon fixation The conversion of carbon dioxide during photosynthesis into such compounds as sugar

carnivore An animal that eats only other animals

chemosynthesis A process by which organisms that do not receive any sunlight, such as those that live in the deep sea, make food using chemicals

commensalism A relationship in which one organism benefits and the other organism is neither helped nor harmed

community A group of living things that live in the same area and interact with each other

competition The demand of two organisms for the same limited resource

condensation The process by which water vapor becomes liquid, usually caused by a drop in air temperature

consumer An organism that obtains its food by eating other organisms, such as plants or animals

deciduous Plants that lose their leaves in fall and remain leafless until spring

decomposer An organism, such as an earthworm, a mushroom, or bacterium, that eats dead animal and plant material

DNA (deoxyribonucleic acid) A large molecule in the nucleus of cells that contains instructions for the genes that make up a cellular form of life

ecosystem A small or large unit of the environment containing a community of organisms; an ecosystem can be as small as a puddle or as large as a mountain.

energy pyramid A diagram indicating how much energy is passed from organism to organism in a food chain

evaporation The process by which a liquid is changed into a gas (or vapor).

first-level consumer A consumer, an herbivore, or omnivore that eats producers

food chain A single path of food energy transfer from one organism to another

food web A group of interconnected food chains resulting in several paths of food energy transfer from organism to organism

habitat An area that supplies a population with everything it needs to survive: food, water, shelter, and space

herbivore An organism that eats only producers or plants; examples are rabbits, deer, and manatees

mutualism A relationship in which both species benefit

niche A region within an ecosystem that includes all of an organism's activities

nitrogen cycle The movement of nitrogen through Earth's ecosystems

nitrogen fixation The conversion of nitrogen gas into nitrogen compounds by means of bacteria in soil or water

omnivore An organism that eats both producers and consumers; examples are bears, raccoons, and wasps

organisms Living plants or animals that carry on life activities

paramecium An elongated single-celled organism that has hairlike edges

parasitism A relationship in which one organism benefits and the other is harmed

photophore A special organ that enables deep-sea fish to produce their own light

photosynthesis A process that enables producers to make their own food

population All the organisms of a single type that inhabit a specific locality

precipitation Water that falls back to Earth as rain, sleet, snow, or hail

primary succession A process by which plants grow where there were no plants before

producer An organism that can make its own food using photosynthesis; examples

are plants, algae, mosses, and phytoplankton

secondary succession A process by which plants start to grow again after they have been removed (for example, by a forest fire)

second-level consumer A consumer that eats first-level consumers

succession A change in an ecosystem's cycle that may bring about a change in species

symbiosis A close relationship between two different species; examples are mutualism, commensalism, and parasitism

toxin A poisonous substance that can be passed from organism to organism up the food chain

water cycle The sequence of conditions by which water passes from vapor through condensation and precipitation and back into the atmosphere by evaporation

FURTHER INFORMATION

Books

Biomes Atlases (series). Austin, TX: Raintree Steck-Vaughn, 2003.

Carson, Rachel. *Silent Spring* (40th anniversary edition). Boston: Houghton Mifflin, 2002.

Carson, Rachel. *The Sea Around Us.* New York: Oxford University Press, 2003.

Ecosystems in Action (series). Minneapolis: Lerner, 2003.

Protecting Habitats (series). Milwaukee: Gareth Stevens, 2004.

Web Sites
Nature Zip Guides
www.enature.com/zipguides

Biomes
www.picadome.fcps.net/lab/currl/biomes/default.htm

Missouri Botanical Gardens
www.mbgnet.net

DVDs/Videos
Underwaterworld: Trilogy (Deep Encounters/Ocean Allies/Blue Voices). Image Entertainment, 2002.

Habitats, Video Learning System 6. FogWare, 2005.

Deserts of the American West. Educational Video Network, Inc., 2004.

Tropical Rainforest. Vista Point Ent., 2005.

INDEX